Annotated Teacher's Edition

H5000013

Write Away SkillsBook

Editing and Proofreading Practice

. . . a resource of student activities
to accompany the *Write Away* handbook

WRITE SOURCE®

GREAT SOURCE EDUCATION GROUP
a Houghton Mifflin Company
Wilmington, Massachusetts

A Few Words About the
Write Away SkillsBook

Before you begin . . .

The *SkillsBook* provides you with opportunities to practice editing and proofreading skills presented in the *Write Away* handbook. The handbook contains guidelines, examples, and models to help you complete your work in the *SkillsBook*.

Each *SkillsBook* activity includes a brief introduction to the topic and examples showing how to complete that activity. You will be directed to the page numbers in the handbook for additional information and examples. The "Proofreading Activities" focus on punctuation, the mechanics of writing, usage, and spelling. The "Sentence Activities" provide practice in sentence combining and in correcting common sentence problems. The "Language Activities" highlight the parts of speech.

Many exercises end with a KEEP GOING activity. Its purpose is to provide follow-up work that will help you apply what you have learned in your own writing.

Authors: Pat Sebranek and Dave Kemper

Printed in the United States of America

International Standard Book Number: 0-669-48237-4 (student edition)

2 3 4 5 6 7 8 9 10 -DBH - 05 04 03 02

International Standard Book Number: 0-669-48238-2 (teacher's edition)

2 3 4 5 6 7 8 9 10 -DBH - 05 04 03 02

Table of Contents

Proofreading Activities

Using Punctuation

Checking Mechanics

Checking Your Spelling

Using the Right Word

Sentence Activities

Language Activities

Nouns

Pronouns

Verbs

Adjectives

Parts of Speech

Theme Word Activities

Theme Words

Proofreading Activities

The activities in this section include sentences that need to be checked for punctuation, mechanics, or usage. Most of the activities also include helpful handbook references. In addition, KEEP GOING, which is at the end of many activities, encourages follow-up practice of certain skills.

Name

_____

Periods as End Punctuation

A **period** is used as a signal to stop at the end of a sentence. Put a period at the end of a telling sentence.

A Put periods at the ends of these telling sentences.

1. Our class lines up at the main door _____•_____

2. Sometimes we make our teacher smile _____•_____

3. We play indoors on rainy days _____•_____

4. There are some great new books in the library _____•_____

5. I like to write funny stories _____•_____

B Write two telling sentences about your school.

1. _____

_____

2. _____

_____

4

C Put a period at the end of each sentence in this letter.

October 10, 2001

Dear Aunt Fran,

    I like school this year. There are 22 kids in my class. A new boy sits next to me. His name is Robert. I think we're going to be friends. I'll let you know in my next letter.

Love,

Timmy

Now answer these questions about the letter.

1. How many telling sentences are in the letter? _____6_____

2. How many periods are in the letter? _____6_____

Name _____

Periods After Abbreviations

Use **periods** after these abbreviations:
Mr., Mrs., Ms., and Dr.

Dr. Green   Mrs. Linn

(**Dr.** is the abbreviation for **doctor**.)

A Put periods after the abbreviations in these sentences. (Some sentences need more than one period.)

1. Mrs. Linn is our teacher.

2. Mr. and Mrs. Linn have three rabbits.

3. Mr. Linn gave the rabbits their names.

4. They are Ms. Hop, Mr. Skip, and Mrs. Jump.

5. Mrs. Linn took the rabbits to Dr. Green for shots.

6. Dr. Green said, "Those are good names!"

7. Mrs. Linn told Dr. Green that Mr. Linn made up

the names.

6

B Write two silly names for rabbits. One name should start with Mr. and one with Mrs. Then write two sentences that use the names.

Name: _Mr._ _____

Name: _Mrs._ _____

1. _____

   _____

   _____

2. _____

   _____

   _____

C Write the names of four grown-ups. Be sure to write Mr., Mrs., Ms., or Dr. before each name.

1. _____

2. _____

3. _____

4. _____

Name

Periods Between Dollars and Cents

Use a **period** (decimal point) between dollars and cents.

$1.50 $3.00 $7.95

A Put periods (decimal points) between the dollars and cents in these sentences.

1. Dan made $4.35 selling lemonade and cookies.

2. I paid $1.50 for two cookies.

3. Dan put $1.35 in his bank.

4. He spent $5.00 for two movie tickets.

5. Tickets only cost $2.50 on Saturday afternoon.

6. My lunch ticket cost $5.00 this week.

7. Ms. Bank paid $3.50 for lunch.

8. I saved $8.00 for my new bike.

8

B Fill in the blanks in the problems below. Remember to use decimal points correctly.

1. $1.00 + $4.00 = _____ $5.00

2. $8.00 − $2.00 = _____ $6.00

3. $3.00 + $3.00 + $3.00 = _____ $9.00

4. $5.00 − $2.00 = _____ $3.00

5. $1.00 + $2.00 + $3.00 = _____ $6.00

6. $4.00 + $1.00 + $1.00 = _____ $6.00

C Write each amount listed below in numerals. Remember to use decimal points correctly.

1. One dollar and fifty cents _____ $1.50

2. One dollar and twenty cents _____ $1.20

3. Five dollars and ten cents _____ $5.10

4. Ten dollars and sixty-nine cents _____ $10.69

5. Two dollars and no cents _____ $2.00

6. Six dollars and fifty cents _____ $6.50

Name _____

Question Marks

Put a **question mark** after a
sentence that asks a question.

What is the longest river?

A **Put a question mark after each sentence
that asks a question. Put a period after
each of the other sentences.**

1. The world's longest river is the Nile ___.___

2. Where is the Nile ___?___

3. The Nile River is in Africa ___.___

4. Are there crocodiles in the Nile ___?___

5. You could jump in and find out ___.___

6. Are you kidding ___?___

7. I'd rather just ask someone ___.___

8. Are you afraid of crocodiles ___?___

9. Who wouldn't be afraid ___?___

B Put a period or a question mark at the end of each sentence in this paragraph.

Lots of animals live in rivers. Of course, fish live in rivers. What else lives in rivers? Snails, frogs, and turtles live in and around rivers. Have you heard of river otters? They are very good at diving. They can stay underwater for four minutes. Do you know any other animals that dive?

Write two questions about rivers. Remember to use question marks!

1. _____

_____

2. _____

_____

Name

Exclamation Points

Put an **exclamation point** after an "excited" word.

Help!

Yuck!

Also put an exclamation point after a sentence showing strong feeling.

Don't touch that!

A Put an exclamation point after each "excited" word and after each sentence that shows strong feeling.

1. I found a treasure map___!___

2. No way___!___

3. It's true___!___

4. Wow___!___

5. Let's find the treasure___!___

6. We'll be famous___!___

7. This could be dangerous___!___

8. I think I see a pirate___!___

B Each of the following sentences needs an exclamation point or a question mark. Put the correct end punctuation after each sentence.

1. Look, Tom, it's a cave ___!___

2. It's dark ___!___

3. It's creepy ___!___

4. Did you see that ___?___

5. What is it ___?___

6. It's a bat ___!___

7. Wow, that's neat ___!___

8. Here we go ___!___

Imagine that you are in a dark cave. Write a sentence that ends with an exclamation point.

_____

_____

Name _____

End Punctuation

Use a **period (.)** after a telling sentence. Use a **question mark (?)** after a sentence that asks a question. Use an **exclamation point (!)** after a sentence that shows strong feeling.

 **Put the correct end punctuation after each sentence.**

(Answers may vary.)

1. Dad's taking us to the ice-cream store ___!___

2. Hooray! Let's have a race to the car ___!___

3. What flavor will Dad choose ___?___

4. He likes hot-fudge sundaes ___.___

5. What do you think Mom wants ___?___

6. She'll probably get frozen yogurt ___.___

7. What should we get ___?___

8. Let's get ice-cream sandwiches ___! (or) .___

B Write a telling sentence, an asking sentence, and a sentence showing strong feeling about your favorite dessert.

Telling Sentence: _____

_____

Asking Sentence: _____

_____

Strong Feeling Sentence: _____

_____

C Ask a partner a question. Write your partner's name, the question you asked, and your partner's answer.

Partner's Name: _____

Question: _____

_____

Answer: _____

_____

Name

_____

End Punctuation Review

Use a **period** after a telling sentence. Use a **question mark** after a sentence that asks a question. Use an **exclamation point** after a sentence that shows strong feeling.

A **Put the correct end punctuation after each sentence.**

(Answers will vary.)

Does this ever happen to you? It's time for bed, but you're not sleepy. You try to lie still. You look around. You just have to get up! You want to get a book or a toy. You try to be quiet. It's hard to see in the dark! You make a loud noise. Someone says, "What's going on in there?" Then you hear, "Get back in bed!"

 **Draw a picture of something you like to do after school.**

 **Write three sentences about your picture. First write a telling sentence. Next write a question. Then write a sentence that shows strong feeling.**

1. Telling Sentence: _____

_____

2. Asking Sentence: _____

_____

3. Strong Feeling Sentence: _____

_____

Name _____

Comma Between a City and a State

Put a **comma** between the name of a city and a state.

Austin, Texas   Salem, Oregon

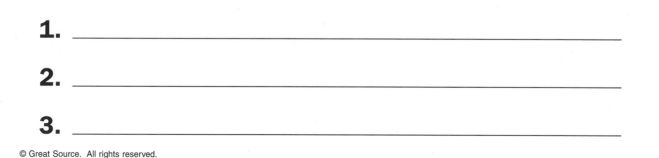

A **Put commas between the cities and states below.**

1. Calumet **,** Michigan

2. Casper **,** Wyoming

3. Williamsburg **,** Virginia

4. Portland **,** Maine

5. Dallas **,** Texas

6. Dayton **,** Ohio

B **Write the names of three cities and states shown on the United States map on page 319 in your handbook. Be sure to put a comma between the name of the city and the state.**

1. _____

2. _____

3. _____

18

Draw a picture of a place in your city or town. Beneath your drawing, write sentences about your picture.

I live in _____

_____

_____

_____

_____

Name

Comma Between the Day and the Year

Put a **comma** between the day and the year.

January 17, 2004
November 12, 2004

December 2004						
S	**M**	**T**	**W**	**T**	**F**	**S**
			1	2	3	4
5	6	7	8	9	10	11
12	13	14	15	16	17	18
19	20	21	22	23	24	25
26	27	28	29	30	31	

 **Look at the calendar on this page. Then write the correct month, day, and year.**

1. Write the date that is circled.

December 12, 2004

2. Write the date that has a diamond around it.

December 25, 2004

3. Write the date for the last day of the month.

December 31, 2004

4. Write the date for the first Monday of the month.

December 6, 2004

B Write the dates for the following days. Be sure to include the month, day, and year. The months are listed on page 260 in your handbook.

1. Your next birthday:

_____

2. Today:

_____

3. Tomorrow:

_____

Write a true or make-believe sentence about the day you were born. Include the date of your birth in your sentence.

_____

_____

_____

_____

Name
_____

Commas in Letters

Put **commas** after the greeting and the closing of a letter.

Dear Grandpa Joe, ← **greeting**
        I love my new fishing rod! Thank you!
Can we go fishing soon? I hope so!
        Love,
        Ben ↖ **closing**

A **Put commas where they belong in these letters.**

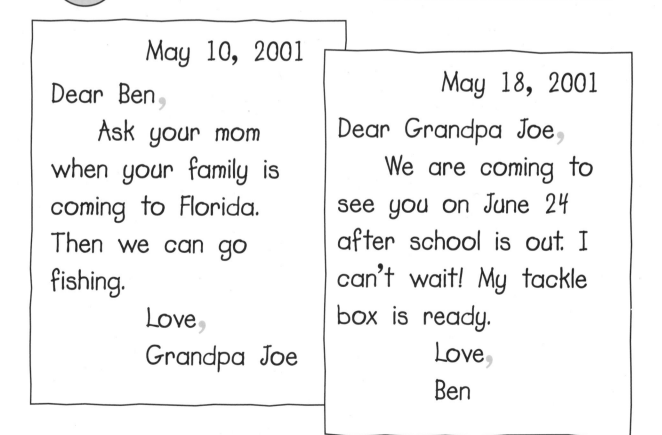

May 10, 2001

Dear Ben,
    Ask your mom when your family is coming to Florida. Then we can go fishing.
        Love,
        Grandpa Joe

May 18, 2001

Dear Grandpa Joe,
    We are coming to see you on June 24 after school is out. I can't wait! My tackle box is ready.
        Love,
        Ben

B Put commas in Grandpa's letter. Then pretend you are Ben. Write what you would say in your next letter to Grandpa Joe. Be sure to put commas in the right places.

May 24, 2001

Dear Ben,

    I will be seeing you in one month! We'll camp out in a tent. We'll have a campfire.

        Love,

        Grandpa Joe

_____

(Date)

_____

(Greeting)

_____

_____

_____

(Closing)

_____

(Signature)

Name

Commas in Big Numbers

Use **commas** to keep big numbers clear.

I said there were 1 0,0 0 0 ants at the picnic.

Mr. Dell said there were only 8,5 0 0.

A **Put a comma where it is needed in each number.**

1. Joey's little brother asks the same question 2,0 0 0 times.

2. Mrs. Roundtree has a book with 1,1 1 7 pages.

3. A crowd of 4,5 0 0 people watched the fireworks.

4. About 1 0,0 0 0 mosquitoes were there, too.

5. Uncle Harry always says, "That's the $6 4,0 0 0 question!"

6. The deepest part of the Pacific Ocean is 3 6,1 9 8 feet deep.

7. Mount McKinley is 2 0,3 2 0 feet above sea level.

8. Angel Falls is 3,2 1 2 feet high.

24

B Open your handbook to page 321. Write a sentence that answers each question. Make sure to use commas correctly in your numbers.

1. How long is the Mississippi River?

The Mississippi River is 2,340 miles long.

2. How high is Mt. McKinley?

Mt. McKinley is 20,320 feet above sea level.

3. How big is the largest desert in the United States?

The Mojave Desert is 15,000 square miles.

4. How big is the largest lake?

Lake Superior is 31,820 square miles.

5. How big is the smallest state?

Rhode Island is 1,214 square miles.

Draw a picture of a mountain. Use your own paper. On your drawing, write a sentence telling how high your mountain is.

Name

Commas Between Words in a Series

Put **commas** between words in a series.

The five senses are sight, hearing, taste, smell, and touch.

A **Put commas where they are needed in these sentences.**

1. Most foods taste sweet, sour, or salty.

2. Smell, sight, and taste help us enjoy food.

3. Almost everybody likes candy, cookies, and cake.

4. Pizza, brownies, and roses smell good.

5. Cats can see only black, white, and gray.

6. Dogs, cats, and bats hear all kinds of sounds.

7. Sounds can be loud, soft, or just right.

8. Teddy bears are soft, cuddly, and fuzzy.

26

B List three or four things in each category below.

My Favorite Tastes	My Favorite Smells	My Favorite Sounds

C Finish the sentences below using words from your lists. Remember to use commas between words in a series.

1. My favorite tastes are _____

_____ and _____ .

2. My favorite smells are _____

_____ and _____ .

3. My favorite sounds are _____

_____ and _____ .

Name _____

Commas to Set Off a Speaker's Words

When you write a speaker's exact words, you may tell who is speaking at the **beginning** of the sentence, or at the **end** of the sentence.

Mr. Kent said, "Kari, you may begin your report."

"My report is on birds," Kari said.

A **Put commas where they are needed in these sentences.**

"Many birds migrate in the winter," Kari said.

Darrin asked, "What does *migrate* mean?"

"Migrate means that some birds go to a new place in winter," Kari answered. She added, "Birds migrate to find food and water."

"That's very interesting," said Mr. Kent.

B Write questions that Bill and Regina might ask about birds and migration. Use question marks and commas correctly.

Bill asked " _____

_____

_____ "

Regina asked " _____

_____

_____ "

List three places you would like to migrate (travel) to.

1. _____

2. _____

3. _____

Name

Comma Review

This activity reviews comma uses you have learned.

 **Put a comma between the names of the cities and the states in these sentences.**

1. You can see mountains from Portland, Oregon.

2. The James River goes through Richmond, Virginia.

3. El Paso, Texas, is near Mexico.

4. Sitka, Alaska, is on the Pacific Ocean.

5. Hilo, Hawaii, is part of an island.

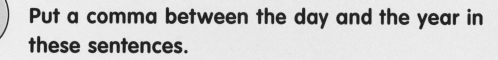 **Put a comma between the day and the year in these sentences.**

1. George Washington was born February 22, 1732.

2. The first nickel was made on May 16, 1866.

3. On February 7, 1867, Laura Ingalls Wilder was born.

4. The astronaut Sally Ride was born May 26, 1951.

C **Put commas between words in a series in these sentences.**

1. Red, orange, yellow, and green are rainbow colors.

2. My uncle, aunt, and cousin live in Michigan.

3. Jonathan likes snowboarding, sledding, and skiing.

4. My family has two cats, one dog, and a turtle.

5. I send letters, notes, and e-mail messages.

D **Put commas where they are needed.**

Maggie asked, "What kind of seashell is that?"

"It's a heart cockle," Molly said. "If you put two

together, they form a heart."

"Amazing!" Maggie added. "What's this one?"

"It's called a turkey wing," Molly answered.

"That's a perfect name! It looks just like one,"

said Maggie.

Name

Making Contractions

A **contraction** turns two words into one word. To make a contraction, put an apostrophe where one or more letters are left out.

Two Words	Contraction
does not	doesn't
he will	he'll

A In the second column, cross out the letters that are left out of the contraction in the first column.

Contraction	Two Words
1. I'm	I am
2. she'll	she will
3. he's	he is
4. they're	they are
5. he'd	he would
6. hasn't	has not
7. we'll	we will
8. shouldn't	should not

32

B **Make contractions from the words below. Remember to use an apostrophe each time!**

1. do not _____don't_____

2. that is _____that's_____

3. cannot _____can't_____

4. I have _____I've_____

C **On each blank below, write the contraction for the words in parentheses.**

1. _____I'm_____ going to make a mask.
  (I am)

2. _____I'll_____ make it out of a paper bag.
  (I will)

3. _____It's_____ going to be a scary mask.
  (It is)

4. Dad _____doesn't_____ know I am making it.
  (does not)

Name _____

Apostrophes in Contractions

A **contraction** turns two words (or one longer word) into one word. To make a contraction, put an apostrophe where one or more letters are left out.

Two Words	Contraction
she will	she'll

A In each sentence, underline the contraction. Then write the word or words the contraction stands for. The first one has been done for you.

1. "Peter <u>didn't</u> obey Mom," said Flopsy. _____did not_____

2. "You <u>can't</u> go to the ball," she told Cinderella.

_____cannot_____

3. "You <u>wouldn't</u> help me," said the Little Red Hen.

_____would not_____

4. "I <u>couldn't</u> sleep in that bumpy bed," said the princess.

_____could not_____

5. The wolf said, "<u>I'll</u> blow your house down." _____I will_____

6. "<u>I'm</u> a real boy!" shouted Pinocchio. _____I am_____

B Write the two words that each contraction stands for. The first one has been done for you.

1. doesn't ___does not___

2. hasn't ___has not___

3. he's ___he is___

4. I've ___I have___

5. isn't ___is not___

6. it's ___it is___

7. we're ___we are___

8. you'll ___you will___

Write a sentence using one of the contractions above.

_____

_____

_____

Name
_____

Apostrophes to Show Ownership

Add an **apostrophe** and an **"s"** to a word to show ownership.

Tom has a boat.   It is Tom's boat.

A   **Each phrase below shows ownership. Draw a picture in each box.**

the cat's rug	the bird's nest
Susan's jump rope	my mother's hat

B **Write the words below to show ownership. Be sure to add an apostrophe and an "s" to each word.**

1. the _____tree's_____ leaves
(tree)

2. the _____kite's_____ string
(kite)

3. the _____airplane's_____ wing
(airplane)

4. the _____bird's_____ tail
(bird)

C **Write the names below to show ownership. Add an apostrophe and an "s" to each name.**

1. I see _____Maria's_____ purple pencil.
(Maria)

2. This is _____Don's_____ math book.
(Don)

3. _____Jane's_____ backpack is heavier than mine.
(Jane)

4. _____Sol's_____ idea notebook is on the desk.
(Sol)

Name

Quotation Marks Before and After a Speaker's Words

Comic strips make it easy to tell who is speaking. They use speech balloons. Here Mom and Steve are talking about dinner.

Mom, can we make pizza for dinner?

That sounds really good to me.

PIZZA MIX

When you write sentences, you use **quotation marks** to show the speaker's exact words.

Steve asked, "Mom, can we make pizza for dinner?"

"That sounds really good to me," Mom said.

A Read the speech balloons. Then write the sentences below. Put quotation marks where they are needed.

Can we make pepperoni pizza?

Sure, but add a vegetable, too.

Steve asked, "Can we make pepperoni pizza?"

_____

Mom answered, "Sure, but add a vegetable, too."

_____

How about mushrooms?

Great choice!

Steve asked, "How about mushrooms?"

_____

Mom said, "Great choice!"

_____

Name

Quotation Marks for Titles

Put **quotation marks** around the titles
of stories and poems.

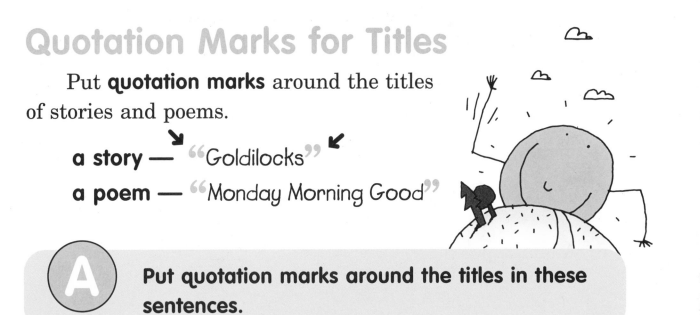

a story — "Goldilocks"

a poem — "Monday Morning Good"

A **Put quotation marks around the titles in these sentences.**

1. "The Tortoise and the Hare" is a fable.

2. "The Ugly Duckling" is my favorite fairy tale.

3. "Eletelephony" is a poem that makes me laugh.

4. I like the poem "Beans, Beans, Beans."

5. We read the fable "The Lion and the Mouse."

6. We read the poem "Oodles of Noodles."

7. Did you read "Rumpelstiltskin" yet?

B Use your handbook to help you fill in each blank with the correct title. Make sure to use quotation marks correctly.

1. The fable _____ "The Wolf, the Gopher, and the Kid" _____

_____ is on page 131.

2. A shape poem called _____ "Clouds" _____ is

on page 151.

3. An add-on story called _____ "Dance Steps" _____

is found on page 127.

4. _____ "Keeping the Dressing" _____ is the all-about-me

story on page 77.

5. A poem called _____ "The Pool" _____ is on page 143.

Write a sentence about a poem or a story you like. Give the title and use quotation marks correctly.

_____

_____

_____

Name

Underlining Titles

Underline the titles of books and magazines.

a book — Onion Sundaes

a magazine — 3, 2, 1 Contact

A **Underline the titles in the following sentences.**

1. My sister's favorite book is Pocahontas.

2. My grandmother has a book called Mrs. Bird.

3. Kids Discover is a magazine for kids.

4. The title of our handbook is Write Away.

5. Ranger Rick is a nature magazine for kids.

6. I just read Ira Sleeps Over by Bernard Waber.

7. My dad reads National Geographic every month.

8. Our teacher is reading All About Sam to us.

B Complete the following sentences. Remember to underline the titles.

1. My favorite book is _____

_____ .

2. My favorite magazine is _____

_____ .

3. The title of the last book I read is _____

_____ .

Draw a cover for one of your favorite books. Write the book title on your cover.

Name

_____

Punctuation Review

This review covers punctuation marks you have learned.

A **Fill in each list below. Use funny or real names.**

Cat Names	City Names	Food Names
1. Buddy	1. _____	1. _____
2. _____	2. _____	2. _____
3. _____	3. _____	3. _____

B **Use your lists to write some funny sentences.**

1. Write a **telling sentence** about three cats.

_____

_____

2. Write an **asking sentence** about three cities.

_____

_____

3. Write an **exciting sentence** about three foods.

_____

_____

C Write contractions for the words below.

1. did not _____didn't_____   **6.** cannot _____can't_____

2. you are _____you're_____   **7.** we have _____we've_____

3. I am _____I'm_____   **8.** has not _____hasn't_____

4. it is _____it's_____   **9.** is not _____isn't_____

5. they will _____they'll_____   **10.** she is _____she's_____

D Fill in each blank with a word that shows ownership.

1. The dog has a ball. It is the _____dog's_____ ball.

2. Alisha has a computer. It is _____Alisha's_____ computer.

3. Our teacher has a bike. It is our _____teacher's_____ bike.

4. Barry has a pet bird. It is _____Barry's_____ pet bird.

Name

Capital Letters to Begin Sentences

Always use a **capital letter** for the first word in a sentence.

We go to the park in the summer.

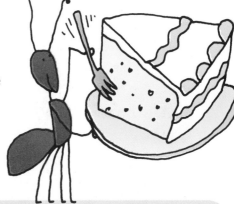

A **Begin each of the following sentences with a capital letter.**

1. One day we had a picnic.

2. aunt Jill brought a big bowl of fruit salad.

3. grandma made lemonade and a chocolate cake.

4. we had sub sandwiches and taco chips.

5. all the kids played softball before lunch.

6. after the game everyone drank lemonade.

7. grandma's cake was the best part of the picnic.

8. the ants liked it, too.

B Put a capital letter at the beginning of each sentence. Put a period at the end of each sentence.

T
X̶here's a swimming pool at our park. S̶ometimes
we go there for a swim. I̶ learned how to swim last
year. N̶ow I can go in the deep end of the pool. M̶y
little sister can't swim yet. S̶he stays in the shallow
end. M̶aybe I'll teach her how to swim.

Write two sentences about things you like to do in the summer. Remember to use capital letters and periods.

1. _____

   _____

2. _____

   _____

Name _____

Capital Letter for a Speaker's First Word

Use a **capital letter** for a speaker's first word.

He asked, "Can you guess what this is?"

A Add capital letters where they are needed.

1. Our teacher asked, "D̶o̶ you know the story of the blind

men and the elephant?"

2. "I̶ do," said Jasmine. "Ȯne man feels the elephant's

trunk. H̶e thinks an elephant is like a big snake."

3. "A̶nother man feels the ear," Kerry added. "H̶e thinks

an elephant is like a big fan."

4. Jasmine said, "A̶nother man feels the leg. H̶e thinks an

elephant is like a tree trunk."

5. Then Ms. Tyler asked, "H̶ow could they know the truth?"

6. Kerry said, "T̶hey could work and talk together."

B Add capital letters where they are needed.

1. Ms. Tyler said, "that's right, Kerry."

2. She asked, "when do you like to work together?"

3. Kerry answered, "i like working together to perform

plays."

4. Jasmine added, "that's something one person can't do

alone."

Complete this sentence telling what the elephant thinks about the blind men.

The elephant said, "_____

_____ ."

Name

Capital Letters for Names and Titles

Use **capital letters** for people's names and titles.

title   **name**

Mr. Thomas lives in a little house.
Mrs. Thomas lives there, too.

A **Add capital letters where they are needed.**

1. Our class helper is ṁrs. ċantu.
M   C

2. The school nurse is ṁr. ṫhomas.
M   T

3. Yesterday, ẇill and I went to see ḋr. ṗaula.
W   D   P

4. I asked ṁs. ḋiGiaimo to read me a story.
M   D

5. Mr. and ṁrs. ċhang picked us up at camp.
M   C

6. Tomorrow, ṁs. ḃanks and ṡally are coming over.
M   B   S

7. Our dentist is ḋr. ṿilla.
D   V

8. After school, ṁr. ċollins helps us cross the street.
M   C

B Draw a picture or paste a photo of your favorite grown-up.

Write two sentences telling why you like this grown-up. Make sure to use the grown-up's title and name each time.

1. _____

_____

2. _____

_____

Name

_____

Capital Letter for "I"

Use a **capital letter** for the word "I."

↗ I have curly red hair.
Cory and I like to tap-dance.

A **Write the word "I" in each of these sentences.**

1. Jimmy and ___I___ are friends.

2. Sometimes ___I___ go to his house.

3. ___I___ ride there on my bike.

4. Sometimes Jimmy and ___I___ play at the park.

B **Write two sentences of your own using the word "I."**

1. _____

_____

2. _____

_____

Draw a picture of yourself in the box below. Then write three sentences about yourself. Use the word "I" in each sentence.

1. _____

_____

2. _____

_____

3. _____

_____

Name

_____

Capital Letters for Book Titles

Most words in book titles begin with **capital letters.**

➤ <u>Town Mouse, Country Mouse</u>

Some words do not begin with capital letters (unless they are the first or last word of a title). Here are some examples:

a   an   the   and   but   of
to   with   by   for   on

A   **Write the four underlined book titles correctly on the lines below.**

    I went to the library yesterday. I found some wonderful books! I checked out <u>my great-aunt arizona</u>, <u>boxcar children</u>, <u>the three sillies</u>, and <u>the new kid on the block</u>.

1. <u>My Great-Aunt Arizona</u>

2. <u>Boxcar Children</u>

3. <u>The Three Sillies</u>

4. <u>The New Kid on the Block</u>

B Interview yourself! Write down the titles of your favorite book and magazine.

Book: _____

Magazine: _____

Write a note telling someone about your favorite book or magazine.

Dear _____ ,

_____

_____

_____

_____

_____

Your friend,

_____

Name

Capital Letters for Days of the Week

Use **capital letters** for days of the week.

Sunday   **W**ednesday

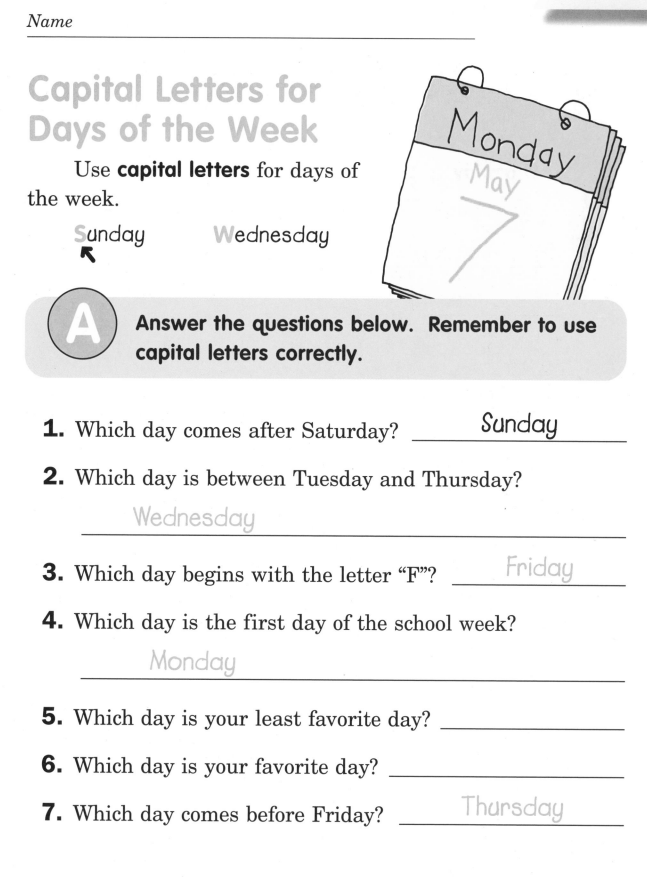

A Answer the questions below. Remember to use capital letters correctly.

1. Which day comes after Saturday? _____ Sunday _____

2. Which day is between Tuesday and Thursday?
_____ Wednesday _____

3. Which day begins with the letter "F"? _____ Friday _____

4. Which day is the first day of the school week?
_____ Monday _____

5. Which day is your least favorite day? _____

6. Which day is your favorite day? _____

7. Which day comes before Friday? _____ Thursday _____

B Put the days of the week in the correct order, starting with Sunday.

Thursday Sunday Tuesday Monday

Friday Wednesday Saturday

1. _Sunday_

2. _Monday_

3. _Tuesday_

4. _Wednesday_

5. _Thursday_

6. _Friday_

7. _Saturday_

Write a sentence about your favorite day of the week.

_____

_____

_____

Name _____

Capital Letters for Months of the Year 1

Use **capital letters** for the months of the year.

February   **M**ay

A Use capital letters for the months in these sentences.

1. The first day of spring is in ~~m~~March.

2. The first day of summer is in ~~j~~June.

3. The first day of fall is in ~~s~~September.

4. The first day of winter is in ~~d~~December.

5. The first month of the year is ~~j~~January.

6. The shortest month is ~~f~~February.

7. Usually ~~j~~July and ~~a~~August are the hottest months.

8. ~~a~~April showers bring spring flowers.

B Here are three more months. Write each month correctly.

may _____ May _____

october _____ October _____

november _____ November _____

KEEP GOING

Write one sentence about each month above.

1. _____

_____

_____

2. _____

_____

_____

3. _____

_____

_____

Name
_____

Capital Letters for Months of the Year 2

Use **capital letters** for the months of the year.

A Read the sentences below. Write the month correctly on the line after each sentence.

1. Handwriting Day is the 12th of january. ___January___

2. Groundhog Day is in february. ___February___

3. Arbor Day is in april. ___April___

4. Memorial Day is the last Monday in may. ___May___

5. My birthday is in june. ___June___

6. Halfway Day is the second of july. ___July___

7. Labor Day is in september. ___September___

8. Fire Prevention Week is during october. ___October___

9. Thanksgiving Day is in november. ___November___

B Unscramble these months and write them correctly on the lines below. Remember to use a capital letter for the first letter!

1. uejn   June

2. gsatuu   August

3. hamrc   March

4. yrjnuaa   January

5. larip   April

6. yma   May

7. tbreoco   October

8. eeedmbcr   December

9. eyfbarru   February

10. ljuy   July

11. ervbnome   November

12. tpbreesme   September

Name

Capital Letters for Holidays

Use **capital letters** for the names of holidays.

Father's **D**ay   **T**hanksgiving **D**ay

 **A** **Use capital letters for the holidays in these sentences. ("Day" is part of many holiday names.)**

1. N̶ew Y̶ear's D̶ay is in January.

2. We made cards for v̶alentine's d̶ay.

3. We celebrate p̶residents' d̶ay in February.

4. m̶other's d̶ay and m̶emorial d̶ay are always in May.

5. One holiday in June is f̶lag d̶ay.

6. July 4 is i̶ndependence d̶ay.

7. The first Monday in September is l̶abor d̶ay.

8. The second Monday in October is c̶olumbus d̶ay.

B Write the names of three holidays that were not found in the sentences on page 61.

1. _____

2. _____

3. _____

Now use the names of those three holidays in sentences.

1. _____

_____

_____

2. _____

_____

_____

3. _____

_____

_____

Name

_____

Capital Letters for Names of Places

Use a **capital letter** for the name of a city, a state, or a country.

City	State	Country
Carson **C**ity	**N**evada	**F**rance
Rome	**I**owa	**C**had

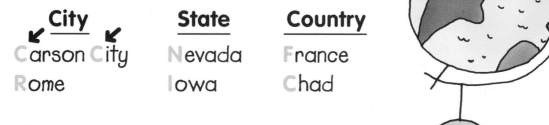

 **A** **Write the city, state, or country correctly in the following sentences.**

1. Make Way for Ducklings takes place in the city of

boston. _____Boston_____

2. The Everglades are in florida. _____Florida_____

3. My grandma is from ireland. _____Ireland_____

4. Mt. Fuji is in japan. _____Japan_____

5. The Sears Tower is in chicago. _____Chicago_____

6. The Peach State is georgia. _____Georgia_____

7. The capital of Alaska is juneau. _____Juneau_____

B Use the map on page 319 of your handbook to answer these questions.

1. Which two states have "South" in their names?

South Dakota

South Carolina

2. Which two states begin with the letter "K"?

Kansas

Kentucky

3. Which three states have only four letters in their names?

Iowa

Ohio

Utah

4. Which state do you live in?

_____

5. Name a state that is near your home state.

_____

6. Which state has four eyes (i's) but cannot see?

Mississippi

Name _____

Capital Letters Review

This activity reviews some of the different ways to use **capital letters**.

A Put capital letters where they are needed. (There are 19 in all.) Watch for these things:
* first word in a sentence,
* names and titles of people, and
* names of cities, states, and countries.

O
X̶ur class is studying rivers.   M̶r. B̶anks read a

book to us about the N̶ashua R̶iver.   T̶he book was

written by L̶ynne C̶herry.   W̶e also learned about the

N̶ile R̶iver in A̶frica.   I̶t is the longest river in the

world.   M̶s. J̶ohnson visited our class.   S̶he went

down the A̶mazon R̶iver on a raft!   S̶he showed

slides of her trip.

> **B** Put capital letters where they are needed.
> (There are 11 in all.) Watch for these things:
>   * a speaker's first word,
>   * names of days and months, and
>   * names of holidays.

1. Joel said, "~~m~~ ^Mmy favorite day is ~~s~~ ^Ssunday. What's

yours?"

2. "~~s~~ ^Ssunday is my favorite day, too," I answered.

3. "~~w~~ ^Wwhat's your favorite month?" Molly asked.

4. I said, "~~m~~ ^Mmy favorite month is ~~j~~ ^Jjuly, because it's

summer, and that's when I was born."

5. Molly said, "~~m~~ ^Mmy favorite month is ~~d~~ ^Ddecember,

because that's when we celebrate ~~h~~ ^Hhanukkah."

6. "~~t~~ ^Tthat's when we celebrate ~~c~~ ^Cchristmas," I said.

> **C** Put capital letters where they are needed in
> these titles.

1. ~~t~~ ^Tthe ~~t~~ ^Ttigger ~~m~~ ^Mmovie   **2.** ~~t~~ ^Tthe ~~f~~ ^Ffox and the ~~h~~ ^Hhound

Name _____

Plurals

Plural means more than one. For most nouns, make the plurals by adding "**s**."

desk ➜ desk**s**   window ➜ window**s**

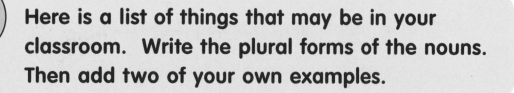

A Here is a list of things that may be in your classroom. Write the plural forms of the nouns. Then add two of your own examples.

1. flag _____ flags _____

2. table _____ tables _____

3. eraser _____ erasers _____

4. pencil _____ pencils _____

5. book _____ books _____

6. marker _____ markers _____

7. door _____ doors _____

8. ruler _____ rulers _____

9. _____ _____

10. _____ _____

B Fill in the blanks by changing the singular word under the line into a plural word.

There are 16 ____girls____ and 10 ____boys____
         (girl)   (boy)

in my class this year. We have one teacher and two

____helpers____ . There are three learning
   (helper)

____centers____ in the classroom. In the reading center
   (center)

there are lots of ____magazines____ . The art center has
              (magazine)

some very bright ____markers____ . In the writing center
               (marker)

there's a whole box of ____pencils____ and many different
                  (pencil)

____kinds____ of paper. I love my classroom!
   (kind)

Write a sentence telling how many boys and girls there are in your class.

_____

_____

_____

Name

Plurals Using "s" and "es" 1

For most nouns, make the **plurals** by adding **"s."**

| one bird | two birds |
| a bike | four bikes |

For some nouns, you need to do more. Add **"es"** to words that end in **sh, ch, s,** or **x**.

| a bush | some bushes |
| one box | two boxes |

A **Write the plurals of the following nouns. It's easy—just add "s."**

1. bug ___bugs___

2. river ___rivers___

3. eye ___eyes___

4. ear ___ears___

5. sister ___sisters___

6. dog ___dogs___

7. house ___houses___

8. desk ___desks___

9. tree ___trees___

10. lake ___lakes___

B Make the following nouns plural. They all end in *sh*, *ch*, *s*, or *x*. That means you need to add "es."

1. brush ____brushes____ **5.** crash ____crashes____

2. class ____classes____ **6.** patch ____patches____

3. bench ____benches____ **7.** boss ____bosses____

4. fax ____faxes____ **8.** bunch ____bunches____

C Fill in each blank with the correct plural. You will need to add "s" to some nouns and "es" to other nouns.

1. At the petting zoo there are baby ____lions____
(lion)

and ____foxes____ .
(fox)

2. There are three ____hamsters____ and
(hamster)

two ____gerbils____ in my classroom.
(gerbil)

3. My mom makes ____lunches____ for me and
(lunch)

my two ____brothers____ .
(brother)

Name

_____

Plurals Using "s" and "es" 2

Make the **plurals** of most nouns by adding "**s**."

one snack   two snacks

For nouns that end in **sh**, **ch**, **s**, or **x**, add "**es**" to make the plurals.

one lunch   two lunches

> **A**   **Write the plurals of the following nouns. Add "s" or "es."**

1. apple   _apples_

2. carrot   _carrots_

3. dish   _dishes_

4. glass   _glasses_

5. spoon   _spoons_

6. box   _boxes_

7. peach   _peaches_

8. sandwich   _sandwiches_

9. raisin   _raisins_

10. cookie   _cookies_

Draw a funny lunchbox on your own paper. Include some of the things you just listed.

72

Name _____

Words That Change to Make Plurals

A few nouns make their **plurals** by changing letters and words. Here are some examples:

child – children   mouse – mice
foot – feet   wife – wives
goose – geese   woman – women
knife – knives   wolf – wolves
man – men

 **A**   **Fill in each blank with the correct plural from the nouns above.**

1. There's a song about three blind _____mice_____ .

2. You clap with your hands and walk with your ____feet____ .

3. Set the table with _____knives_____, forks, and spoons.

4. Ducks and _____geese_____ like to swim in ponds.

5. Sheep need to be protected from _____wolves_____ .

6. Cartoons are for _____children_____, but_____men_____

and _____women_____ watch them, too.

7. Husbands have _____wives_____ .

Name

Plurals of Words That End in "y" 1

Here are two rules for making **plurals** of nouns ending in **"y"**:

Rule 1 If there is a vowel right before the **"y,"** just add **"s."**

turkey   turkeys

Rule 2 If there is a consonant right before the **"y,"** change the **"y"** to **"i"** and add **"es."**

puppy   puppies

A **Make the following nouns plural using rule 1 or rule 2.**

1. story   stories

2. candy   candies

3. donkey   donkeys

4. key   keys

5. baby   babies

6. day   days

B Here are some more nouns that end in "y." Write their plurals. Be sure to check the letter before the "y."

1. monkey _monkeys_

2. lady _ladies_

3. fly _flies_

4. toy _toys_

5. kitty _kitties_

6. battery _batteries_

7. holiday _holidays_

8. bay _bays_

Circle three of the plurals you just made. Use each one in a sentence.

1. _____

_____

2. _____

_____

3. _____

_____

Name

Plurals of Words That End in "y" 2

Some words end with a consonant and "**y**." To make their plurals, change "**y**" to "**i**" and add "**es**."

one baby ➔ two babies

one story ➔ two stories

A Write the plurals of the following nouns. Use the rule you just learned.

1. cherry _cherries_

2. kitty _kitties_

3. party _parties_

4. French fry _French fries_

5. guppy _guppies_

6. bunny _bunnies_

7. pony _ponies_

8. puppy _puppies_

9. country _countries_

10. worry _worries_

On your own paper, draw a picture of some of the animals you just listed.

76

Name _____

Plurals Review

This activity reviews making **plurals**.

A **Make these nouns plural by adding "s" or "es."**

1. glass _____glasses_____   **4.** bus _____buses_____

2. brush _____brushes_____   **5.** dress _____dresses_____

3. frog _____frogs_____   **6.** worm _____worms_____

B **Make these nouns plural by adding "s" or changing "y" to "i" and adding "es."**

1. monkey _____monkeys_____   **4.** turkey _____turkeys_____

2. puppy _____puppies_____   **5.** toy _____toys_____

3. day _____days_____   **6.** cherry _____cherries_____

C **Change these words to make them plural.**

1. mouse _____mice_____   **3.** woman _____women_____

2. foot _____feet_____   **4.** knife _____knives_____

Name

Abbreviations

Put a **period** after a person's title.

Mr.   Mrs.   Ms.   Dr.

Ms. Walters   Mr. Johnson

A **Put periods after the people's titles in these sentences.**

1. Mr. Forest is our next-door neighbor.

2. Mr. and Mrs. Forest have a very big garden.

3. Mrs. Forest works in her garden on cool mornings.

4. Her friend Dr. Maynard stops to visit before work.

5. Mrs. Forest gives Dr. Maynard some pretty flowers to take to the office.

6. After dinner, Mr. Forest likes to weed the garden.

7. Mrs. Forest helps him water the plants.

B Think of four people who work in your school. Write their names below. Be sure to write Mr., Mrs., Ms., or Dr. before each.

1. _____

2. _____

3. _____

4. _____

Choose two of the people. Write a sentence about each person.

1. _____

_____

2. _____

_____

Name

_____

Abbreviations for Days and Months

When writing sentences, you should write the full names of the days and the months.

Today is Tuesday, October 9.

You should also know the **abbreviations** for the names of the days and the months.

Tuesday ➡ Tues.   October ➡ Oct.

A   **Write the abbreviations for the days and months in the following lists.**

1. Sunday _____Sun._____

2. Friday _____Fri._____

3. Wednesday _____Wed._____

4. Thursday _____Thurs._____

5. Saturday _____Sat._____

6. Monday _____Mon._____

7. February _____Feb._____

8. March _____Mar._____

9. November _____Nov._____

10. August _____Aug._____

11. September _____Sept._____

12. January _____Jan._____

80

Name
_____

Post Office Abbreviations

First study the "Post Office State Abbreviations" with a partner, if your teacher says it is okay. Then close your handbook.

 **Draw a line from each state to its post office abbreviation.**

1. California	CO
2. Colorado	FL
3. Florida	KS
4. Illinois	CA
5. Kansas	IL
6. Massachusetts	TX
7. Michigan	NC
8. New York	MI
9. Texas	MA
10. North Carolina	NY

Name _____

Checking Mechanics Review 1

This activity reviews some of the ways to use capital letters.

(A) **Put capital letters where they are needed. There are 22 for you to find.**

D
dear tim,

    how are you? how is life in florida? today ms. martinez said she wished we could all visit you. i told her i get to visit you in june!

    i just read a book called the magic paintbrush. it is a good story from china. lee gave me the book for christmas.

    mrs. james said she hopes you like your new school. do you?

                  Your friend,

                  roger

B Fill in the blanks below. Use your handbook if you need help.

1. Write two days of the week that are school days:

_____   _____

2. Write the name of a holiday: _____

3. Write your first name: _____

4. Write the name of a planet: _____

5. Write your teacher's name: _____

Now use the words you just wrote to complete this story.

It was _____ , but there was no school. It
(day of the week)

was _____ . _____ had a busy
(name of the holiday)   (teacher's name)

day planned. _____ was going to build a
(your name)

spaceship and blast off to _____ .
(planet)

Name

Checking Mechanics Review 2

This activity reviews plurals and abbreviations.

A **Write the plural of each animal name.**

1. cow _____cows_____

6. mouse _____mice_____

2. donkey _____donkeys_____

7. fox _____foxes_____

3. finch _____finches_____

8. pig _____pigs_____

4. goose _____geese_____

9. puppy _____puppies_____

5. guppy _____guppies_____

10. turkey _____turkeys_____

B **Write the abbreviation for each day of the week.**

1. Monday _____Mon._____

5. Friday _____Fri._____

2. Tuesday _____Tues._____

6. Saturday _____Sat._____

3. Wednesday _____Wed._____

7. Sunday _____Sun._____

4. Thursday _____Thurs._____

C **Write the abbreviations for the months of the year.**

1. January   Jan.

2. February   Feb.

3. March   Mar.

4. April   Apr.

5. May   May

6. June   Jun.

7. July   Jul.

8. August   Aug.

9. September   Sept.

10. October   Oct.

11. November   Nov.

12. December   Dec.

Name

ABC Order

Words in **alphabetical (ABC) order** are listed by their first letter in the order of the letters of the alphabet.

 apple   banana   cherry   date

A **Rewrite this list of names. Put them in alphabetical order.**

Ben	**1.**	Adam
Ethan	**2.**	Ben
Danielle	**3.**	Chris
Will	**4.**	Danielle
Richard	**5.**	Ethan
Adam	**6.**	Isabelle
Vanessa	**7.**	Maria
Isabelle	**8.**	Richard
Chris	**9.**	Vanessa
Maria	**10.**	Will

B Write down the first names of seven students in your class. Each name should begin with a different letter. First write the names in the order you think of them. Then write the names in ABC order.

Any Order	ABC Order
1. _____	1. _____
2. _____	2. _____
3. _____	3. _____
4. _____	4. _____
5. _____	5. _____
6. _____	6. _____
7. _____	7. _____

Write a sentence that names one boy and one girl in your class.

_____

_____

Name

Sorting Nouns

A **noun** names a person, a place, or a thing.

Person	Place	Thing
girl	tree house	egg

A Sort the words in the box into three groups: words that name people, words that name places, and words that name things.

sister	park	computer	zipper	apple	baby
uncle	table	family	forest	zoo	school

People Words

1. sister
2. uncle
3. family
4. baby

Place Words

1. park
2. forest
3. zoo
4. school

Thing Words

1. table
2. computer
3. zipper
4. apple

B Draw a picture that shows one of the place words.

Write a sentence or two telling about your picture. Underline the place words.

_____

_____

Name

Sorting Nouns and Verbs

A **noun** names a person, a place, or a thing.

Dalton   mall   cat

A **verb** shows action or helps complete a thought.

throw   are   have

Sort the words in the box into two groups: nouns and verbs.

sun	is	melts	brother	Grand Canyon
howled	has	was	Paula	classroom

Nouns

1. sun
2. classroom
3. Paula
4. Grand Canyon
5. brother

Verbs

1. howled
2. is
3. has
4. melts
5. was

B Write two sentences. In each sentence, use one noun you listed and one verb you listed.

1. _____

_____

2. _____

_____

 Draw or find a picture to go with one of your sentences.

Name

_____

Sorting Long "a" Words and Long "e" Words

A long **a** sound is the vowel sound you hear in **cake, train,** and **day**.

A long **e** sound is the vowel sound you hear in **street, heat,** and **see**.

A Sort the words in the box into two groups: words that have the long "a" sound and words that have the long "e" sound.

sea	face	beak	snail	bee	snake
leap	ape	chase	spray	green	chief

Long "a" Sound	Long "e" Sound
1. face	1. sea
2. ape	2. leap
3. chase	3. beak
4. snail	4. bee
5. spray	5. green
6. snake	6. chief

B Each word pair has either the long "a" sound or the long "e" sound. Write which sound each word pair has.

1. green bee _____long e_____

4. whale tail _____long a_____

2. flea feet _____long e_____

5. sleepy beast _____long e_____

3. grape ape _____long a_____

6. stray snail _____long a_____

Draw a picture that shows one of the word pairs. Then write a silly sentence about your picture.

Name

Using the Right Word 1

Some words sound alike, but they have different spellings. They also have different meanings. (These words are **homophones**.) Here are some examples:

I **hear** you.   I am **here**.

A   **Fill in each blank with "here" or "hear."**

1. I asked my dog Dan to come _____ here _____ .

2. Can you _____ hear _____ what I am saying?

3. Did you _____ hear _____ what happened to Sara?

4. _____ Here _____ is the ball I thought I lost.

5. I _____ hear _____ music.

6. Dan can _____ hear _____ better than people.

B   **Write a sentence using "hear" and "here."**

_____

_____

C Read the example sentences using "no" and "know." Then fill in each blank with the correct word.

Anna said, **"No** thanks."
I **know** about computers.

1. There is _____*no*_____ more ice cream.

2. I _____*know*_____ where to get some.

3. Just answer yes or _____*no*_____ .

4. Do you _____*know*_____ the new girl?

5. I don't _____*know*_____ her yet.

6. There is _____*no*_____ school tomorrow.

D Write a sentence using "no" and "know."

_____

_____

Name

_____

Using the Right Word 2

Some words sound alike, but they have different spellings. They also have different meanings. (These words are **homophones**.) Here are some examples:

These shoes are new.   I knew the answer.

A   **Fill in each blank with "new" or "knew."**

1. I got a _____new_____ raincoat.

2. My mom _____knew_____ it was going to rain today.

3. My sister got _____new_____ boots.

4. Dave wrote a _____new_____ story.

5. Mike said he _____knew_____ how it would end.

6. We start a _____new_____ chapter today.

B   **Write a sentence using "new" and "knew."**

_____

_____

C Read the sentence using "sea" and "see." Then fill in each blank with the correct word.

I would like to **see** a whale in the **sea**.

1. In my dream, I was swimming in the _____sea_____ .

2. I could _____see_____ under the water.

3. I saw a huge _____sea_____ monster.

4. I could _____see_____ its big, sharp teeth.

5. I didn't want to _____see_____ it up close.

6. Now I don't like to swim in the _____sea_____ !

KEEP GOING

Write a sentence using "sea" and "see."

_____

_____

_____

Name

Using the Right Word 3

Some words sound alike, but they have different spellings. They also have different meanings. (These words are **homophones**.) Here are some examples:

I have **two** cats.
I have a dog, **too**.
I go **to** Pine Elementary.

A **Fill in each blank with "two," "to," or "too."**
"Too" can mean "also" or "more than enough."

1. We are going _____ to _____ the beach.

2. We can only stay for _____ two _____ hours.

3. Can Marla come, _____ too _____ ?

4. I like to take a radio _____ to _____ the beach.

5. Just don't play it _____ too _____ loud.

B **Write a sentence using "two" and "to."**

_____

_____

C **Read the sentence using "read" and "red."**
Then fill in each blank with the correct word.

I read my **red** notebook.

1. The U.S. flag is _____*red*_____ , white, and blue.

2. Our class _____*read*_____ about the flag.

3. Candy canes are _____*red*_____ and white.

4. Our teacher uses a _____*red*_____ pen.

5. Casey _____*read*_____ his story to the class.

6. Tina _____*read*_____ a poem.

D **Write a sentence using "read" and "red."**

_____

_____

Name
_____

Using the Right Word 4

Some words sound alike, but they have different spellings. They also have different meanings. (These words are **homophones**.) Here are some examples:

We saw their new puppy.
("Their" shows ownership.)

There are three pets now.

They're lots of fun.
(*They're* = they are.)

A **Fill in each blank with "their," "there," or "they're."**

1. _____There_____ are four kids in the Clark family.

2. We play freeze tag in _____their_____ backyard.

3. _____They're_____ my next-door neighbors.

4. _____Their_____ mother loves animals.

5. Sometimes _____they're_____ busy feeding the pets.

6. _____There_____ are messes to clean up, too!

B Write three funny sentences using at least two of these words in each sentence: "their," "there," and "they're."

1. _____

_____

2. _____

_____

3. _____

_____

C Draw a picture for one of your funny sentences.

Name

Using the Right Word Review 1

This activity reviews the **homophones** you have practiced.

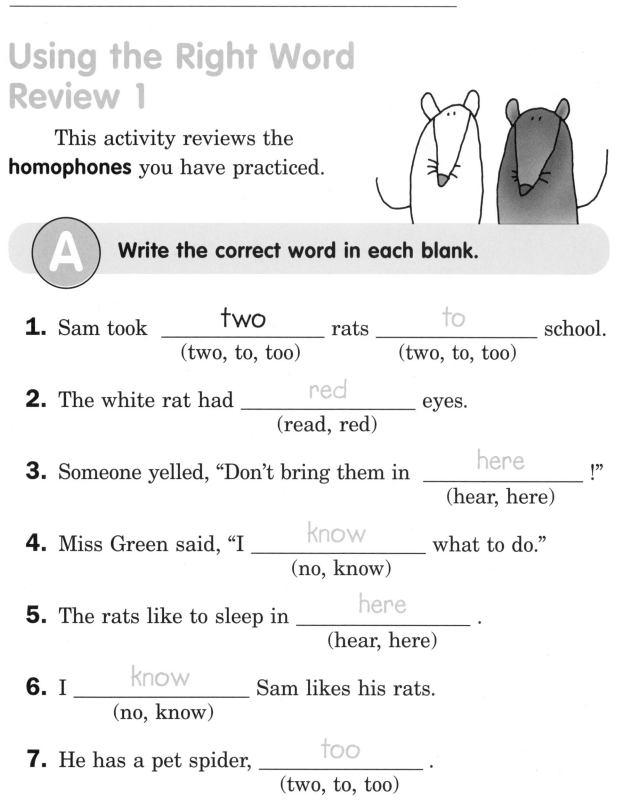

A **Write the correct word in each blank.**

1. Sam took ____two____ rats ____to____ school.
(two, to, too)   (two, to, too)

2. The white rat had ____red____ eyes.
(read, red)

3. Someone yelled, "Don't bring them in ____here____!"
(hear, here)

4. Miss Green said, "I ____know____ what to do."
(no, know)

5. The rats like to sleep in ____here____ .
(hear, here)

6. I ____know____ Sam likes his rats.
(no, know)

7. He has a pet spider, ____too____ .
(two, to, too)

8. Don has a _____new_____ pet parrot.
(new, knew)

9. _____There_____ are more than 300 kinds of parrots.
(Their, There, They're)

10. First he _____read_____ all about parrots.
(read, red)

11. Then he _____knew_____ how to take care of one.
(new, knew)

12. You should _____hear_____ the parrot talk!
(hear, here)

 **B** Write three sentences. Use one of these words in each sentence: "to," "two," "too."

1. _____

_____

2. _____

_____

3. _____

_____

Name

Using the Right Word Review 2

**Before each sentence is a group of words.
Choose the correct word to fill in each blank.**

1. (hear, here) "Did you __hear__ that Uncle Andy

and Aunt Sue are coming __here__ ?" I asked.

2. (know, no) "Oh, __no__ , I didn't __know__

that," Lea answered.

3. (read, red) "They got a little __red__ sailboat," I

said. "I __read__ about it in Uncle Andy's letter."

4. (their, there, they're) "I hope __they're__ bringing

__their__ boat when they come," Lea said.

5. (knew, new) "Sure," I said. "They __knew__ we'd

want to sail in the __new__ boat."

B Below are three homophone pairs. Pick one pair, and draw a picture showing those words. (Use your handbook if you need to check meanings.) Then write a sentence about your picture.

ant aunt   ate eight   dear deer

Sentence Activities

This section includes activities related to basic sentence writing, kinds of sentences, and sentence problems.

Name _____

Understanding Sentences

A **sentence** tells a complete thought.

This is not a complete thought:
On the window.

This is a complete thought:
A bug is on the window.

A Check whether each group of words is a complete thought or not.

	Complete Thought	
	Yes	**No**
1. From the downstairs music room.		✓
2. The sound was very loud.	✓	
3. Covered his ears.		✓
4. After that.		✓
5. He shut the front door.	✓	
6. Max played the drums.	✓	
7. Ming played the piano.	✓	
8. Mom the silver flute.		✓

B Fill in each blank with a word that completes the thought.

1. _____ was playing with a ball.

2. The _____ rolled down the hill.

3. _____ ran after it.

4. Then a big, hairy _____ ran after it, too.

5. The _____ got the ball and kept running.

6. Was the _____ gone for good?

Draw a picture about sentence 4.

Name

_____

Parts of a Sentence 1

Every **sentence** has two parts, the **subject** and the **verb**.

<u>Joe</u> <u>planted</u> a seed.

subject ↗   ↖ verb

The subject is the naming part. The verb tells what the subject is doing.

 **Underline the subject with one line. Underline the verb with two lines.**

1. <u>Joe</u> <u>watered</u> his seed every day.

2. <u>He</u> <u>watched</u> it carefully.

3. A tiny <u>leaf</u> <u>popped</u> out.

4. The <u>leaf</u> <u>grew</u> larger.

5. A <u>flower</u> <u>bloomed</u> one morning.

6. <u>Joe</u> <u>told</u> his mom.

7. <u>Mom</u> <u>smiled</u> at Joe.

8. <u>Joe</u> <u>gave</u> the flower to his Mom.

B Write a verb for each sentence.

1. Mom _____ cookies.

2. I _____ her.

3. I _____ the eggs.

4. I _____ the bowls.

5. Mom _____ the cookies in the oven.

6. I always _____ the first cookie.

C Check whether the underlined word is a subject or a verb.

	Subject	Verb
1. Your body <u>has</u> a lot of bones.		✓
2. Your longest <u>bone</u> is in your leg.	✓	
3. Your ribs <u>look</u> like a cage.		✓
4. Your smallest <u>bone</u> is in your ear.	✓	
5. <u>Jellyfish</u> have no bones.	✓	
6. A <u>skeleton</u> is all bones.	✓	

Name

Parts of a Sentence 2

Every **sentence** has two parts, the **subject** and the **verb**.

Haley came to the party.
subject↗   ↖ verb

The subject is the naming part. The verb tells what the subject is doing.

A | **Fill in each blank with a word from the box. You may use some words more than once.**

Poems	Ms. Day	Sam	Tacos
Eddy	Winter	Roses	Sarah

(Answers will vary.)

1. _____ plays on the soccer team.

2. Last summer, _____ drove to Ohio.

3. _____ grow in Grandpa's garden.

4. _____ are my favorite food.

5. _____ sleeps in his doghouse.

6. _____ brings snow and ice to Minnesota.

B Read each sentence in section A again. The word you added is the subject.

C Fill in each blank with a word from the box. You will use each word only once.

learned	barked	is	went
hit	sang	eats	gave

1. Bobby _____ *hit* _____ a home run.

2. The dog _____ *barked* _____ loudly.

3. Steve _____ *eats* _____ toast every morning.

4. Our teacher _____ *gave* _____ us a test.

5. Kerry _____ *sang* _____ a song for the class.

6. At camp, Cheri _____ *learned* _____ to ride a horse.

7. My sister's name _____ *is* _____ Gail.

8. We all _____ *went* _____ for a hike yesterday.

D Read each sentence in section C again. The word you added is the verb.

Name

Kinds of Sentences 1

A **telling sentence** makes a statement. Put a period after a telling sentence.

Buster is out in the rain.

An **asking sentence** asks a question. Put a question mark after an asking sentence.

Where is Buster?

A Write "T" before each telling sentence, and put a period after it. Write "A" before each asking sentence, and put a question mark after it.

_A_ **1.** What is Sandy doing?

_T_ **2.** Sandy is making a bird feeder.

_A_ **3.** Why is she doing that?

_T_ **4.** She wants to see what kinds of birds will come.

_A_ **5.** Where will she put the bird feeder?

_T_ **6.** She's going to hang it in a tree.

_A_ **7.** What kind of food will she put in it?

_T_ **8.** Sandy bought some birdseed for her feeder.

B Draw a picture of some birds at a bird feeder.

Write one telling sentence and one asking sentence about your picture.

1. Telling Sentence: _____

_____

_____

2. Asking Sentence: _____

_____

_____

Name

Kinds of Sentences 2

A **telling sentence** makes a statement. Put a period after a telling sentence.
I'll feed Buster.

An **asking sentence** asks a question. Put a question mark after an asking sentence.
Would you feed Buster, please?

 **Write a telling sentence that is an answer for each asking sentence. Make sure you write complete sentences.**

(Answers will vary.)

1. What happened to your shoes?

_____

2. Who left the door open?

_____

3. How did you get all muddy?

_____

4. Have you read Too Many Tamales?

_____

B Pretend that you are only four years old. Write some asking sentences that a four-year-old might ask. Two examples have been done for you.

1. Where do bugs come from?

2. Why does it get dark at night?

3. _____

4. _____

5. _____

Pick two questions from above. Write telling sentences to answer them. (Write interesting answers that are complete sentences!)

1. _____

_____

2. _____

_____

Name

Sentence Review

This reviews what you have learned about sentences.

A **Write "S" after each sentence. Write "X" after each group of words that is not a sentence.**

1. My dad and I. _____X_____

2. Went to Blue Hills Park. _____X_____

3. We hiked to the top of a big hill. _____S_____

4. Above the clouds! _____X_____

5. Then Treasure Cave. _____X_____

6. It was scary and dark inside. _____S_____

7. Later, we saw three fat raccoons. _____S_____

8. We had a lot of fun. _____S_____

9. Will visit the park again. _____X_____

B **Read page 62 in your handbook to see how the writer made each group of words a complete thought.**

C Underline and label the subjects and verbs in the sentences that begin with "I." The first sentence has been done for you.

Dear Grandma,

Guess what? $\underset{S}{\underline{I}} \underset{V}{\underline{lost}}$ another tooth! $\underset{S}{\underline{I}} \underset{V}{\underline{bit}}$ into an apple.

$\underset{S}{\underline{I}} \underset{V}{\underline{feel}}$ the new hole in my mouth now.

Mom will bring me to your house next week. $\underset{S}{\underline{I}} \underset{V}{\underline{like}}$

your yard. $\underset{S}{\underline{I}} \underset{V}{\underline{think}}$ your new slide is great!

Will you bake cookies for me? See you soon.

Love,

John

 Copy one asking sentence and one telling sentence from the letter.

1. Asking Sentence: _____

_____

2. Telling Sentence: _____

_____

Language Activities

The activities in this section are related to the parts of speech. All of the activities have a page link to *Write Away*. In addition, KEEP GOING, which is at the end of many activities, encourages follow-up practice of certain skills.

Name

Nouns

A **noun** names a person, a place, or a thing.

Person	Place	Thing
student	park	cake
friend	mall	candle

A Write what each noun is: "person," "place," or "thing." Add three nouns of your own.

1. firefighter   person

2. library   place

3. hammer   thing

4. teacher   person

5. pencil   thing

6. store   place

7. _____   _____

8. _____   _____

9. _____   _____

122

B Write "N" if the word is a noun. Write "X" if the word is not a noun.

_N_ **1.** paper   _X_ **4.** bring   _X_ **7.** and

_X_ **2.** go   _N_ **5.** girl   _X_ **8.** hot

_N_ **3.** bee   _N_ **6.** store   _N_ **9.** kite

C Underline the noun in each sentence.

1. The <u>bus</u> is yellow.

2. The <u>spider</u> jumped.

3. This <u>game</u> is hard.

4. Look at the <u>duck</u>!

5. The <u>sky</u> looks pretty.

6. A <u>friend</u> called.

Write a sentence about your favorite toys. Then underline the nouns in your sentence.

_____

_____

_____

Name

Singular and Plural Nouns

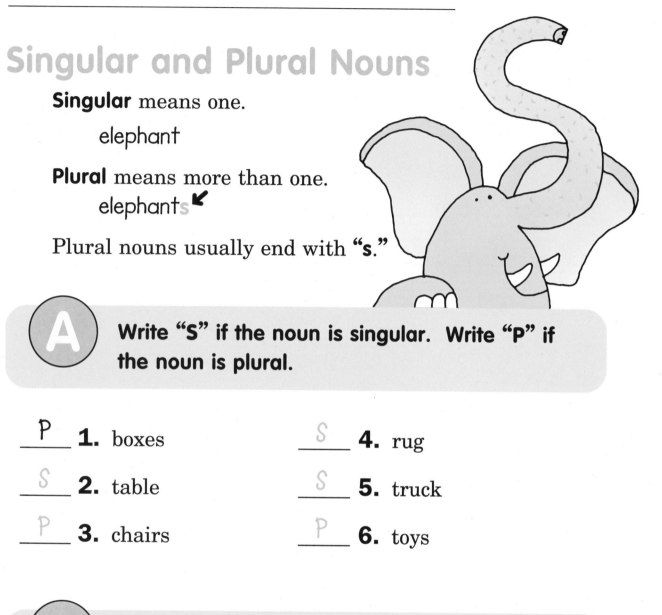

Singular means one.

elephant

Plural means more than one.
elephants

Plural nouns usually end with **"s."**

A **Write "S" if the noun is singular. Write "P" if the noun is plural.**

___P___ **1.** boxes   ___S___ **4.** rug

___S___ **2.** table   ___S___ **5.** truck

___P___ **3.** chairs   ___P___ **6.** toys

B **Write "S" if the underlined noun is singular. Write "P" if the underlined noun is plural.**

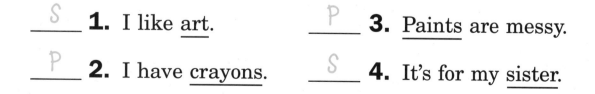

___S___ **1.** I like <u>art</u>.   ___P___ **3.** <u>Paints</u> are messy.

___P___ **2.** I have <u>crayons</u>.   ___S___ **4.** It's for my <u>sister</u>.

C Underline the plural noun in each sentence.

1. The cow has black and white <u>spots</u>.

2. Some <u>piglets</u> are pink.

3. <u>Potatoes</u> spilled out of the grocery bag.

4. My sister baked chocolate chip <u>cookies</u> yesterday.

5. Tony took off his muddy <u>shoes</u>.

6. Erin held the tiny <u>kittens</u>.

Draw a picture about one of the plural nouns you underlined. Write the noun under your picture.

Name

_____

Common and Proper Nouns 1

A **common noun** tells what a thing is.
A **proper noun** tells a thing's name.

Common Noun	Proper Noun
boy	Tony Prada
school	Hill Elementary
city	Lexington

A proper noun begins with a capital letter.
Some proper nouns are more than one word.

A   **Underline the common noun in each sentence.**

1. The <u>class</u> is busy writing.

2. The <u>teacher</u> likes to help.

3. The <u>girl</u> is reading quietly.

4. The <u>street</u> is shiny and wet.

5. The sandy <u>beach</u> is hot.

6. Let's swim in the <u>pool</u>!

7. My <u>puppy</u> is furry and brown.

8. He has a red <u>collar</u>.

B **Underline the proper noun in each sentence.**

1. We stopped at <u>Jefferson Library</u>.

2. <u>Susie</u> wanted a book about horses.

3. This book is about <u>President Lincoln</u>.

4. <u>Principal Brown</u> visited the library.

5. He speaks <u>Spanish</u>.

6. <u>Rosa Perez</u> does, too.

C **Write "C" if the underlined word is a common noun. Write "P" if the underlined word is a proper noun.**

_C_ **1.** My neighbor walks her <u>dog</u> each afternoon.

_P_ **2.** My neighbor's name is <u>Mrs. Lee</u>.

_C_ **3.** Her <u>dog</u> likes me.

_P_ **4.** <u>Alf</u> is a funny dog.

_C_ **5.** One day he got on a <u>bus</u>.

_C_ **6.** The bus <u>driver</u> said, "No dogs on the bus!"

Name

Common and Proper Nouns 2

A **common noun** tells what a thing is. A **proper noun** tells a thing's name.

Common Noun	Proper Noun
holiday	New Year's Day
country	Mexico

A proper noun begins with a capital letter. Some proper nouns are more than one word.

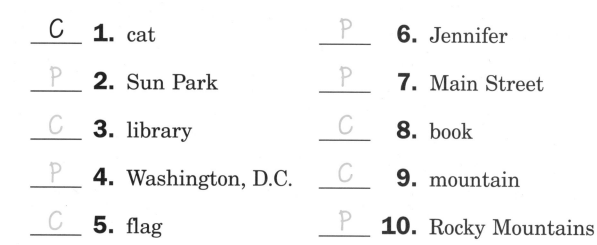

A   **Write "C" if the word is a common noun.**
Write "P" if the word is a proper noun.

__C__ **1.** cat

__P__ **2.** Sun Park

__C__ **3.** library

__P__ **4.** Washington, D.C.

__C__ **5.** flag

__P__ **6.** Jennifer

__P__ **7.** Main Street

__C__ **8.** book

__C__ **9.** mountain

__P__ **10.** Rocky Mountains

128

B **Draw a line from each common noun to the proper noun that fits with it.**

1. girl   United States

2. boy   Fluffy

3. cat   "The Three Bears"

4. country   Tom

5. story   Lisa

C **Write "C" if the underlined noun is a common noun. Write "P" if the underlined noun is a proper noun.**

_P_ **1.** Today is <u>Christmas</u>!

_C_ **2.** There is no <u>school</u> today.

_C_ **3.** The <u>air</u> is freezing cold.

_P_ **4.** <u>Aunt Lizzie</u> visited us.

_C_ **5.** Kevin brought ribbon <u>candy</u>.

_P_ **6.** He is from <u>Korea</u>.

Name

Possessive Nouns

A **possessive noun** shows ownership.
A possessive noun has an **apostrophe**.

Tia's toy boat was left out in the yard.
(The toy boat belongs to Tia.)

After the storm, we found it in the dog's house.
(The house belongs to the dog.)

A **Circle the possessive nouns.**

1. (Mike's) story about Mr. Bug was fun to read.

2. Mr. (Bug's) house was flooded when it rained.

3. When a toy boat floated by, Mr. (Bug's) 148 children

hopped in.

4. All the little Bugs waited for the (storm's) end.

5. Finally the boat floated to a (dog's) house.

6. The (dog's) name was Buddy.

7. The little Bugs asked if they could share their new

(friend's) home.

8. The (story's) title is "The Bugs Find a Buddy."

B Draw a picture of one of these things from the story:

  ✳ Bug's flooded house,
  ✳ the child's toy boat, or
  ✳ the dog's house.

Write a sentence telling about your picture. Use a possessive noun. (Remember to use an apostrophe.)

_____

_____

Name

Pronouns 1

A **pronoun** is a word that takes the place of a noun.

Noun	**Pronoun**
Todd did it.	He did it.
Sally laughed.	She laughed.
The rope broke.	It broke.
The skates are too big.	They are too big.

A **Circle the pronouns that replace the underlined nouns in the sentences below.**

1. <u>Holly</u> gave Katy a Mexican coin.

Ⓢⓗⓔ gave Katy a Mexican coin.

2. Katy put the <u>coin</u> in a safe place.

Katy put ⓘⓣ in a safe place.

3. <u>Peggy and Jo</u> wanted to see the coin.

Ⓣⓗⓔⓨ wanted to see the coin.

4. Then <u>Jay</u> asked to see it, too.

Then ⓗⓔ asked to see it, too.

B Draw a line from each noun to the pronoun that could replace it.

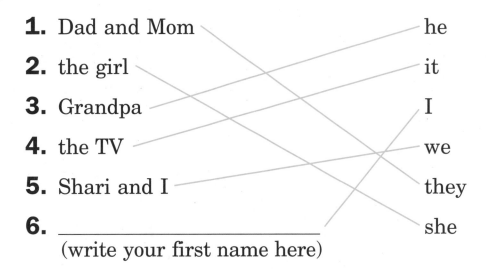

1. Dad and Mom   he

2. the girl   it

3. Grandpa   I

4. the TV   we

5. Shari and I   they

6. _____   she
    (write your first name here)

C In each sentence, write a pronoun to replace the noun. If you need help, check the list of pronouns on page 280 in your handbook.

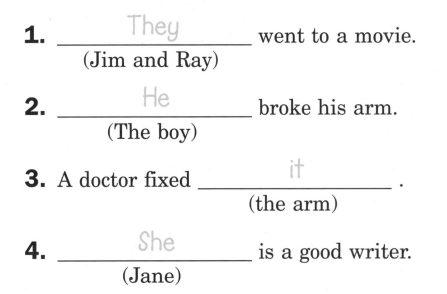

1. _____They_____ went to a movie.
    (Jim and Ray)

2. _____He_____ broke his arm.
    (The boy)

3. A doctor fixed _____it_____ .
        (the arm)

4. _____She_____ is a good writer.
    (Jane)

Name

Pronouns 2

A **pronoun** can take the place of a possessive noun. A possessive noun shows ownership.

Noun	**Pronoun**
Jan's bicycle	her bicycle
Dave's skateboard	his skateboard
the bird's wing	its wing
Mike and Laura's poem	their poem

A **Circle the pronouns that take the place of the underlined nouns in the sentences below.**

1. <u>Juanita's</u> coat is hanging up.

(Her) coat is hanging up.

2. At the picnic, <u>Jake's</u> lunch fell into the water.

At the picnic, (his) lunch fell into the water.

3. Yesterday <u>Sam and Sarah's</u> bus left early.

Yesterday (their) bus left early.

4. The <u>dog</u> was very excited.

(It) chewed on a big bone.

134

B Underline the pronoun in each sentence. Draw a picture of the pet rat.

1. Here is <u>my</u> pet rat.

2. Dad likes <u>its</u> pink ears.

3. Mom likes <u>its</u> long tail.

4. Bogart is <u>our</u> favorite pet.

5. <u>He</u> has red eyes.

6. Ted pets <u>his</u> white fur.

7. <u>We</u> bought a blue cage.

C Draw a line to the pronoun that could replace the underlined words.

1. I heard <u>Tim and Judy's</u> song.　　　　ours

2. I know <u>your sister's</u> name.　　　　Its

3. Here comes <u>Ricky's</u> friend.　　　　their

4. <u>The book's</u> cover got wet.　　　　his

5. The tree house is <u>yours and mine</u>.　　　　her

Name

_____

Pronouns 3

A **pronoun** is a word that takes the place of a noun.

Jason made a sandwich.
Then he ate it.
(The pronouns "he" and "it" take the place of the nouns "Jason" and "sandwich.")

 Fill in each blank with a pronoun that replaces the underlined word or words.

1. Joe and Ann read a poem. ___They___ read it aloud.

2. Tanya drew a map. ___She___ showed it to me.

3. My brother and I have a clubhouse. ___We___ made it ourselves.

4. I hope you're coming to my party. ___It___ will be fun.

5. Mom heard our music. ___It___ was too loud.

6. Tony is coming over. ___He___ is my friend.

7. The monkeys at the zoo played baseball. ___They___ were funny.

8. This book is great. ___It___ has good pictures, too.

B Use each pronoun in a sentence.

I	we	she	they

1. _____

2. _____

3. _____

4. _____

C Draw a picture to go with one of your sentences.

Name _____

Action Verbs

There are different kinds of **verbs**.
Some verbs show action:

Mom found our jump rope.
She gave it to us.

A   **Underline the action verb in each sentence.**

1. Al <u>brings</u> the rope.

2. Eli and Linda <u>hold</u> the rope.

3. They <u>twirl</u> the rope.

4. The other kids <u>count</u> for Al.

5. Scott's dog Stripe <u>barks</u> at Al.

6. Sometimes Al <u>jumps</u> 100 times!

7. Then Linda <u>takes</u> a turn.

8. Mother <u>waves</u> from the window.

9. She <u>points</u> at Stripe.

10. The kids <u>laugh</u>.

138

B Here are some more action verbs. Fill in each blank with a verb from this box.

dive	point	pop
roars	visit	eat

1. Paul and Ann _____*visit*_____ the zoo.

2. They _____*point*_____ at some lions.

3. One of the lions _____*roars*_____ at them.

4. The elephants _____*eat*_____ lots of peanuts.

5. The polar bears _____*dive*_____ into the pool.

6. Prairie dogs _____*pop*_____ out of their tunnels.

Write a sentence about the zoo. Use an action verb.

_____

_____

_____

Name _____

Action and Linking Verbs

Action verbs show action. Here are some examples:

kick   tell   throw   ask   run   write

Linking verbs complete a thought or an idea. Here are some examples:

am   was   is   were   are   be

A **Write "A" if the underlined verb is an action verb. Write "L" if the verb is a linking verb.**

__A__ **1.** Soccer players <u>kick</u> the ball.

__A__ **2.** Football players <u>throw</u> the ball.

__L__ **3.** I <u>am</u> cold.

__A__ **4.** Pat and Rob <u>run</u> around the track.

__L__ **5.** She <u>is</u> a fast runner.

__L__ **6.** They <u>are</u> both in second grade.

__A__ **7.** He <u>paints</u> pictures.

__L__ **8.** Pete and Joni <u>were</u> sick.

B Pick five action verbs from the list on page 283 in your handbook. Use each action verb in a sentence.

1. _____

_____

2. _____

_____

3. _____

_____

4. _____

_____

5. _____

_____

 KEEP GOING

Write a sentence using the linking verb "am."

_____

_____

Name

Verbs: Present and Past Tense

A verb that tells what is happening now is called a **present-tense verb**.

Sean **is** in second grade.
He **takes** swimming lessons every week.

A verb that tells what happened in the past is called a **past-tense verb**.

Last year he **was** in first grade.
He **learned** to play soccer.

A **Check whether each underlined verb is in the present tense or the past tense.**

	Present Tense	Past Tense
1. Bobby <u>broke</u> his leg last weekend.		✓
2. He <u>fell</u> out of a big tree.		✓
3. Now he <u>has</u> a cast on his leg.	✓	
4. He <u>is</u> home from school this week.	✓	
5. Yesterday I <u>took</u> him his homework.		✓
6. I <u>wrote</u> my name on his cast.		✓
7. Bobby <u>walks</u> with crutches.	✓	

B Complete the following sentences. Write the present-tense verb or the past-tense verb in the blank. The first one has been done for you.

Present Tense

1. Now Mom _____makes_____ my lunches for school.
  (makes, made)

2. Now I _____am_____ eight years old.
  (am, was)

3. The sidewalk _____gets_____ slippery when it snows.
  (gets, got)

4. Now Stanis _____takes_____ swimming lessons.
  (takes, took)

Past Tense

1. Last week I _____walked_____ to school with Hector.
  (walk, walked)

2. Yesterday Lydia _____wrote_____ a letter to her aunt.
  (write, wrote)

3. Last summer our family _____went_____ camping.
  (goes, went)

4. This morning I _____was_____ late for school.
  (am, was)

Name

Adjectives 1

An **adjective** describes a noun or a pronoun. An adjective often comes before the word it describes.

Megan has long hair.
Randy wears a black cap.

Sometimes an **adjective** comes after the word it describes.

Parrots are colorful.

A Underline the adjective that describes each circled noun.

1. Elephants are <u>huge</u> (animals.)

2. Their (skin) is <u>wrinkled</u>.

3. Their <u>ivory</u> (tusks) are <u>long</u> (teeth.)

4. Elephants use their <u>floppy</u> (ears) as <u>giant</u> (fans.)

5. An elephant's trunk works as a <u>useful</u> (tool.)

6. It can pick up <u>small</u> (peanuts.)

7. A <u>cool</u> (river) is an elephant's <u>favorite</u> (place.)

B Fill in each blank with an adjective that describes the circled noun.

(Answers will vary.)

1. Elephants make _____ (noises.)

2. Elephants have _____ (trunks.)

3. They have _____ (feet.)

4. Elephants can carry _____ (loads.)

5. Would you take a _____ (ride) on an

elephant?

6. How would you get on a _____ (elephant?)

C Underline each adjective that describes the circled pronoun.

1. (You) are smart.

2. (He) is funny.

3. (They) look tired.

4. (I) am hungry.

5. (It) is green.

6. (We) are cold.

7. (She) feels sick.

8. (They) taste stale.

Name

Adjectives 2

An **adjective** describes a noun or a pronoun. An adjective often comes before the word it describes.

The hungry bear sniffed the berries.

Sometimes an **adjective** comes after the word it describes.

The bear was hungry.

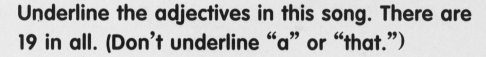

A Underline the adjectives in this song. There are 19 in all. (Don't underline "a" or "that.")

I'm going to tell you a story about a <u>grizzly</u> bear.

It's just a <u>little</u> story about a <u>grizzly</u> bear.

It was a <u>great</u> <u>big</u>, <u>grizzly</u>, <u>grizzly</u> bear.

a <u>great</u> <u>big</u>, <u>grizzly</u>, <u>grizzly</u> bear.

Mama ran away from that <u>grizzly</u> bear.

So daddy went a-hunting for that <u>grizzly</u> bear.

He had <u>long</u>, <u>long</u> hair that <u>grizzly</u> bear.

He had <u>big</u> <u>blue</u> eyes that <u>grizzly</u> bear.

B Write one more sentence for "The Grizzly Bear Song." Underline the adjectives you use.

_____

_____

C Write two sentences using adjectives from the box below. Try using more than one adjective in your sentences.

hairy	purple	loud	cold
dizzy	smelly	squeaky	soft
windy	wet	sweet	sour
chewy	sleepy	strong	goofy

1. _____

_____

2. _____

_____

Name

_____

Articles

The words **"a,"** **"an,"** and **"the"** are **articles**.

Use **"a"** before a consonant sound.

a kite

Use **"an"** before a vowel sound.

an ocean

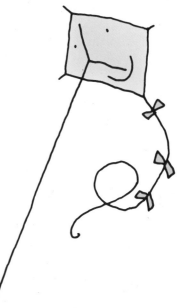

A **Write "a" or "an" before the following words.**

_____an_____ **1.** attic

_____a_____ **2.** chicken

_____a_____ **3.** shovel

_____an_____ **4.** elephant

_____a_____ **5.** tooth

_____a_____ **6.** giant

_____a_____ **7.** dinosaur

_____an_____ **8.** apple

_____a_____ **9.** spider

_____a_____ **10.** whale

_____a_____ **11.** shadow

_____an_____ **12.** envelope

_____an_____ **13.** idea

_____a_____ **14.** monkey

_____an_____ **15.** orange

_____a_____ **16.** package

_____a_____ **17.** kettle

_____an_____ **18.** inchworm

B Fill in the word "a" or "an" in the spaces below.

One day ___a___ spider with yellow feet climbed to the top of ___a___ slide. The slide was in ___a___ park. Soon the spider heard ___a___ radio playing her favorite song. The song was ___an___ old tune called "The Eensy Weensy Spider." The spider began to tap her eight yellow feet. ___An___ inchworm heard the music, too. He inched his way over to the slide and began to tap all of his feet. What ___a___ funny sight to see! ___A___ spider and ___an___ inchworm were dancing in the park.

Draw a picture of the spider and the inchworm.

Name _____

Parts of Speech Review 1

This activity is a review of the parts of speech you have practiced: **nouns (N), pronouns (P), verbs (V),** and **adjectives (A)**.

We ate nice hot soup for lunch.
P   V   A   N

 **What part of speech is underlined in each sentence? Write "N," "P," "V," or "A" in the blank.**

___A___ **1.** A <u>toasted</u> <u>cheese</u> sandwich is <u>great</u>.

___V___ **2.** It <u>smells</u> buttery and <u>looks</u> golden brown.

___V___ **3.** When I <u>bite</u> into it, I <u>see</u> the melted cheese.

___N___ **4.** Toasted cheese <u>sandwiches</u> taste crunchy on the <u>outside</u> and creamy in the <u>middle</u>.

___P___ **5.** My mom makes <u>them</u> on the griddle.

___P___ **6.** <u>I</u> could eat one every day!

___N___ **7.** I hope we have toasted cheese <u>sandwiches</u> for <u>dinner</u> tonight.

___A___ **8.** It would be a <u>super</u> way to end my day.

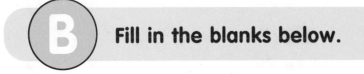

150

B   Fill in the blanks below.

1. Write the name of your favorite food (noun):

_____

2. Write a word that describes it (adjective):

_____

C   Fill in each blank with a word that is the correct part of speech.

1. _____ likes tuna sandwiches.
       (noun)

2. _____ like tacos better.
      (pronoun)

3. I _____ two tacos every day.
     (verb)

4. I like them with _____ cheese.
               (adjective)

5. Sandra's mom _____ the best tacos.
              (verb)

6. She puts _____ sauce on them.
        (adjective)

Name

Parts of Speech Review 2

Do this activity with a partner. (It's about sushi, a special Japanese cold rice cake.)

A **Label all the nouns "N" and the pronouns "P."**

          N   P   N
1. Yesterday Mom and I went to the Japanese grocery store.

  P   N   N
2. We bought raw tuna and salmon.

       N   N   N
3. This morning Mom cooked the rice.

      N P   P   N
4. With a flat spoon, I spread it on the seaweed.

  P   N   N
5. We can add avocados and mushrooms, too.

B **Label all the verbs "V" and the adjectives "A."**

     V   A   A
1. We added orange carrots and green spinach.

     V   V   A
2. As I rolled it together, I squeezed the yummy sushi.

    A   V   A
3. With a sharp knife, Mom cut the roll into small pieces.

     V   A   A
4. Then we poured dipping sauce into tiny bowls.

     V A   A
5. We also ate thin slices of pickled ginger.

C Think of a song or poem you know. Write down at least four lines from it. (You could use a poem you wrote, or one from your handbook.)

_____

_____

_____

_____

_____

_____

_____

_____

In the lines above, find and label two nouns and two verbs. Also label any pronouns and adjectives.

Name

_____

Theme Words

Lists of **theme words** can help you choose and spell interesting words for your writing.

A **Think of a favorite topic. Then list your own theme words below.**

Topic: _____

B Write three sentences that use one or more of your theme words.

1. _____

_____

2. _____

_____

3. _____

_____

Make a picture about one theme word that names something.